ANOTHER LAST DAY

ALSO BY ALEX LEMON

Poetry
The Wish Book
Fancy Beasts
Hallelujah Blackout
Mosquito

Nonfiction
Feverland: A Memoir in Shards
Happy: A Memoir

ANOTHER LAST DAY

poems   Alex Lemon

MILKWEED EDITIONS

Published 2019 by Milkweed Editions
Printed in the United States of America
Cover design by Mary Austin Speaker
Cover photo courtesy of Alex Lemon
19 20 21 22 23   5 4 3 2 1
First Edition

Milkweed Editions, an independent nonprofit publisher, gratefully acknowledges sustaining support from the Ballard Spahr Foundation; the Jerome Foundation; the McKnight Foundation; the National Endowment for the Arts; the Target Foundation; and other generous contributions from foundations, corporations, and individuals. Also, this activity is made possible by the voters of Minnesota through a Minnesota State Arts Board Operating Support grant, thanks to a legislative appropriation from the arts and cultural heritage fund, and a grant from Wells Fargo. For a full listing of Milkweed Editions supporters, please visit milkweed.org.

Library of Congress Cataloging-in-Publication Data

Names: Lemon, Alex, author.
Title: Another last day : poems / Alex Lemon.
Description: First edition. | Minneapolis, Minnesota : Milkweed Editions,
[2019].
Identifiers: LCCN 2018046191 (print) | LCCN 2018054244 (ebook) | ISBN
9781571318442 (ebook) | ISBN 9781571314512 (pbk. : alk. paper)
Classification: LCC PS3612.E468 (ebook) | LCC PS3612.E468 A56 2019 (print) |
DDC 811/.6--dc23
LC record available at https://lccn.loc.gov/2018046191

Milkweed Editions is committed to ecological stewardship. We strive to align our book production practices with this principle, and to reduce the impact of our operations in the environment. We are a member of the Green Press Initiative, a nonprofit coalition of publishers, manufacturers, and authors working to protect the world's endangered forests and conserve natural resources. *Another Last Day* was printed on acid-free 30% postconsumer-waste paper by Versa Press.

for Alma

♥

all hurricane, all heart

I do not know who put me in the world, nor what the world is, nor what I myself am. I am in terrible ignorance of everything. I know not what my body is, nor my sense, nor my soul.

—BLAISE PASCAL

Perhaps that's what I feel, an outside and an inside and me in the middle, perhaps that's what I am, the thing that divides the world in two, on the one side the outside, on the other the inside, that can be as thin as foil, I'm neither one side nor the other, I'm in the middle, I'm the partition, I've two surfaces and no thickness, perhaps that's what I feel, myself vibrating, I'm the tympanum, on the one hand the mind, on the other the world, I don't belong to either.

—SAMUEL BECKETT

ANOTHER LAST DAY

I

all this time
death has refused

to take me & now
when the willows

darken from my chest rips
a flame-winged black–

bird my bones knot
with goodbyes breaking

to not be a carousel
       whirring darkly

II

ambulance lights
in the distance throb

my blood & in my guts
I feel my home

on fire
my family

singing ablaze
from fire-curtained

windows—*we are good*
we are good—they croon

but it is too late always
            now too bright

III

forever along the river
it is a hot hot gust

today I welcome
fat raindrops welcome

whirlwind & hello coming
       darkness where am I

IV

sun-bleached mannequins
rise into the sky

from the bruised water
empty birdcages bend

low the lilacs
a torn orange dress

I long ago yearned to
wear laces the brambles

without knowing
what I am

      I go

V

when I look down
there is nothing

of me but a ragged duffel
bag sinking into the shallows

two babies are zipped up in it
or just one baby

besides me
it is suffocating

in here it is dark
I would be anything else

sunflower black ice
prickly pear

this life of heat
waving apparitions

I am tumbling king
protea pothole

I am asleep I
        am drowning

VI

in the parking lot
a thousand hisses punch

above me in the hot wind
the lights burr on

night puckers with blinks
inside my chest

there is a flowering fist
an empty can herky-jerks

across the humid-slick asphalt
I too am a glassbreak hum

from the coal black beyond
the blinding lights

suddenly falls wet
      sizzling needles

VII

the drizzle makes
the pearled darkness

all around me
terrible & lovely

soon it is pouring
I have never wanted

anything
growing

puddles perfectly swallow
the gloaming the murk

fluttering with thousands
of tiny mouths roaring

silver-lipped water wells
            opening away

VII(Echo)

with my heart
absent in the morning

I walk long staring
overturned sofa on the playground

gutted stuffing clotheslined
from chain link to hydrant

a radiance of cigarette butts
on the cracked sidewalk

squirrel skull on a swing
a mop of yarn clump-floating

the mucky creek
it is a bonfire sinking

a sewage-tattered wig
wisping

shrouded below it
in the brackish water

I know
the rest

of me slumps
a pock-faced zombie

trudging the pitch-black
rocky bottom the silt

with grub-white legs
flesh tearing away in flags

skin nibbled at
by rainbow trout by catfish

by hatchets of pike
all day I follow it follow myself

downstream
telling the gusting wind

about the way things are
in this life—

a body dropped
from the hand

into a pot of boiling water
will balloon

with moisture become so soft
the flesh will hold

the shape of anything
that presses into it—

a hand the ghost of a jellyfish
goodbye lines skin

      etched by a swimsuit

VIII

any day now will come a flood
of bees

coat hangers untwist
from the low branches

fire ants Haitian cockroaches
scurrying the strand

there is not enough time to sit
outside of a door chalked

on the trunk of a tree
there are voices singing inside

no time to be awake always
listening

the sunflowers lean & twist
   through each other

IX

I only want to sleep hard
in the little things I believe

in tennis shoes nailed
to each apple tree

in the garden
the gunked ground

puddled with mirrors
of water

glimmering exits
        from this world

X

before me the weeping
bottlebrush

cradle the air
dark red with flowers

shadow-spidered limbs
oil-black bulbs

hang inside them
dangle & water-skim

from the boughs
all the day around me

sucks into them & soon almost
      nothing remains

XI

an unnameable glut twirls
through my blood

I watch fingertips of light
shear the murk toward noon

the rain turning velvet soft
the day ungloving suddenly

inside out with sunshine
that tangerines the puddles

pulpy & abuzz
with storm gatherings

inside me there is a clump of pearls
an unquenchable want

to take in as much as possible
before the air heaves immense

from me
cavernous & unbreathable

before this wet earth before
these hands this sickness before

me sickles of light in the air
       everywhere sliced with sun

XII

the songs of invisible children
wheel from the thicket

buckling the creekside
I clamber

each gust
the sweetgrass barks

invisible hands rattle
the brambles

at the sky right then
it is almost dark

my legs go mealy
open-mouthed dollheads

hang from the blue
ash limbs stare

pit-eyed & bleached
like forgotten birdfeeders

baggies of sewer
water fly-hearted

pears my throat cottons
does anyone else

ever see what I do
there is nobody here

in the swirling black
a tarantella

where did all of you
leave to where did you

go hear it now do you
          it's so very close

XIII

this unbruising morning
the stars are gemmed turtles

inching around a steel-blue bathtub
everything below the mottled sky

is burnt-toast black
my surround sound crunching

through the brittle grass
here it is not any day

it is all time now
before sunup the ghosts

of the long dead
molder high & gauzy

in the branches above
I cannot move my arms

to cover my eyes to wave goodbye
to say hello come close

to press a palm
to my spring-loaded heart

I cannot move cannot move
endlessly I am stunned

each time I see a flaring
in the knobbed–limb shine

XIV

inside me antlers
lightning

smelted iron pours
through my veins until

there are cages inside me
steel cobwebs woven

through bone inside me
when I cross the bridge

behind my closed eyes
the rising water below

silvers & fumes & deepens
inside me a sputter & gulp

from what lives in there
diamond tumbleweed the lifeless

musicbox with birds & beasts
all the bad weather

behind my eyes
but here the lowing wind

dries this noose of sweat
the knotty branches

hasp along the shoreline
I can see forever

down the empty road
beside no cars no people

no one
it is so good

with only the whispering
dirt of everything

that has come
before & what grows inside

me before too long
            will be light

XV

in the dark woods
a sliver of light

like an eye
opens to a clearing

a dirt baseball field
at home plate a pony

on its side lies motionless
a boy in just underwear

sits repeating his parents' names
a doorless Toyota pickup

half-buried in the loam
nosedown a possum

back & forths
over its rusted roof

I whistle loud & louder
but the truck the boy the possum

don't look up
nothing stops

what it is set
on doing

until a long while later
when I cannot remember

where I am how I got
here my own name

can only hear the electric
churn of a city I do not see

looking around I am alone
now climbing the outfield fence

when a low jet contrails
an expanding arrow across

the heat-smeared blue

XVI

what have you done
with yourself

the wind whistles
through the empty playground

that appears out of nowhere
in a field of moldering corn

what is beautiful
pouched bursts

of trumpet vine
rope the cage of the jungle gym

from them grow purple flowers
the size of fists

the down here dark
the gusts lisp

through the overgrown sward
I feel a shipwreck in my guts

the deepening shade
of the too-tall grass

will wait always
the down here dark

blade-tipped brambles
grow higher around me

just above the flaking schoolyard rubble
I see just barely the sun

it is orange yellow orange
good luck my friend

the monkeybar steel
pings as if slapped by hands

swinging an invisible body
toward me closer & closer

there is no one
when I close my eyes

I feel blindness caving in
          the tumbling sky

XVII

behind my closed eyes
I am driving a car

that has no steering wheel
only an array of doll arms & squirt guns

hundreds of them lined up
along the dash as

I pull triggers & shake
tiny plastic hands the car

veers from roadside to ditch
the radio turns on wipers swoosh

the seat cages around me
the car speeds

around me apparitions
of all of the people I love

fade in & out around me
unsmiling they flicker & glow

around me go out
in the rearview mirror

only to flashbulb
back into being

I mash the brake pedal
lift & lever the arms

but I don't know anything
beyond the serpentine careen

a sudden plunge into dark
in my guts it is oilslick & silent

until the plummet
like a sudden sunrise

begins to bleach
the falling stars

soon the blankness throbs
I am again awake or half

so an all-swallowing white
canvas above me the ceiling

with some beast
from the other side

of myself about to rip
through me into

the slaughterhouse
      of day

XVIII

looking out
from the city's edge

the inferno dusk
over the domed hills perfectly

landscaped over the old dump
makes me need a jean jacket

of waxed denim
with patches of bands

that I have heard play
only in my head

above the immaculate mounds
pinholes throb

the dead refuse to be left
underground

sooner or later
all of my insides

will drop out of me
my pockets will turn

into wind
around whatever becomes

of my bones a few dimes
a museum pin will ping & bound

until they don't
the air thick & still

no industrial-strength zipper
no stretch of taut & unwrinkled skin

will anymore be able
   to contain all of this

XIX

when I finally arrive
at the moan-packed & whispering

emergency room to see
how the people are

truly doing
a splayed-open stepladder

squats beneath an open panel
of humming fluorescent lights

in the ceiling
everyone here

is holding tightly
to someone's hand

except me
I crawl out

of my skin
taste the wind

howling open
I watch

the breaks & sickness & failing
around me

get replaced by more
failing & sickness & breaks

so long & still
the ladder sits untouched

as if unseen by all the illness
the aluminum rungs

begin calling out
so I clap my hands

softly against my thighs
I climb it

rising like an apparition
I float I do not feel

the bones the muscle the blood
in my legs up here

everyone looks delicate & confused
inside them I see

jellyfish
I want to kiss

each of their sick mouths
breathe into them

but there are beehives
uncrowding from

the recessed ceiling & inside
me I know I cannot stay

much longer here
no matter how I might

wish to give them
　　　　all that I have & am

XX

crumpled red in the mouth
of the golden Lab

that saunters into the street
from between two cars

in the parking lot
is a severed hand

glinting between its teeth
in the dark

watching from the sidewalk
I am dumbstruck

all things end in violence
in the city

because you cannot love
everyone enough cannot love

anyone as much as they need
as much as they deserve

the sharp-ribbed dog sits
back on its haunches

in the middle of the street
spotlit by a slowing car

it crouches in front
of the stopping car

whips its head
back & forth

I am filled
with a blood-warm glow

spilling over
with a blood-warm glow

I am rivering I am watching
there is a hollowing-out

hunger inside me
            I could eat god

XXI

the silverflamed husks
of insects scurry around

me over thigh-piled garbage
bags dragged to the curb

for tomorrow's trash pickup
a soiled mattress torn window

screen coiled rug
I sit in the fetid black

mound in a rocking chair
a racketing cloud

of flies above me
blocks out the moon

beneath my tongue
there is a wet convulsion

passing cars blur
the night purple

it is just another night
for them they will say nothing

is wrong over & again
         if even they wonder at all

XXII

the bleak orchard
of the city bleeds

so this glass-shard lot
this cracked kiddie pool

filled wet with sawdust & clumps
of hair a voice that floats up

from the muck I listen
to it I say *hello*

again & again
on the other side

of the poolscum
a boy stands

next to a lawn chair
pyramided with cat

heads each night I see
him in my yard he gives me

a handful of yellow
molars into the fluttering

black he drifts
rising from the murk

    bubbles pop

XXIII

lying in the outside dark
I slapbox the ghosts

of my ragged breath
they are pearl-lipped

outside of me
I sing

to everything
there is no sleep

in this life from my back
every twisting star

up there dead for ages
      looks lovely

XXIV

in the auditorium
of midnight

a white-irised man
sits cross-legged

in the center of the street
while above the dank light

hum darkening ribs of black
from my porch

night is a mansion
of grinning

ghosts a knife
clatters to the pavement

from his hands
my face breaks

into weeping
I want to clap

but only cough
while he stands

jumps into the air
then starts running

harder & harder
        in place

XXV

before the orchestra
in the elm trees

sets down the wind
there are times

I press my hand
to the bloodsweet

emptiness in bed
where moments before

a body was sleeping
& it feels like the coming

undone of this life
       will never happen

XXVI

with the brilliant glint
of a knife-tip

I conduct
the air-scribbling black

flies through morning's
             mottled glow

XXVII

over the drying sidewalk
my face beads with sweat

in the humid air the day
already filling with dust

of the living with the long
gone aches of bones I stop

at each pool left over
from morning's downpour

I want to stomp
in each puddle

but cannot move
the moment I see

myself in the glassed
        black below

XXVIII

glaze-faced with held breath
I watch three butterflies

wing cavities of light
through the day's last sunbeam

a good friend tells me
anything a person might need

can be found
in the sweetmeat

jellied inside
their bones

who would care I asked
if right now all of it

just ended
below the parade of clouds

we watch
a wicked spindling

in the elm's twisted braches
an unmoving shadow

at the neighbor's upstairs window
        a hand spiderlegging the glass

XXIX

what is this place I ask
each day stalking

the cracked-apart streets
I name the skulls

of passersby
sunskirt traceberry

ever-numbed the river
because I know

that music
flesh line-dotted

with a purple marker
a road map

for the cutting
but can't spit

out the words
I am carved hollow

my insides rotted
out whistling my sick

heart down
      the unstitching street

XXX

in the rotting bark
a termite's jaws write

that all of the pills
are long gone long gone

then carves out my name
before gnawing an X

through it
I can no longer speak

about sword swallowing or love
how someday we might rise

nude in the backyard sunlight
after a night of rain

the elm tree is leafed
with gunked-up old photos

I say god good god
            to the face in each

XXXI

after the dark drops
with birds bleating

in the branches
I huff dreadstruck

in the throat
wanting so badly

to believe
that someone

will take
care of us

when the marl comes
dying to taste

the last little bite
       of our singing

XXXII

I am always lost
in the sunflowered distance

between myself & gasping
for breath

against an orange construction fence
I old-man lean

giving up
on the run

kicking the dandelions
that line the gravel road

down
while I but I might I

just now I want
to tear my heart

out & feed it
to the mangy dog

who has all day swung
his close wet nose

after my heel

XXXIII

after the rain
the leech sheen

grows flawless
thousands

of them
are bandaged

around the tree
I wish I was

more afraid
to remember

what I look like
I have to press

my fingers
into my face

all the nailheads
   shine like eyes

XXXIV

as the sky lowers
I loop knots of rope

around the ceiling beams
of the porch

because each hummingbird
feeder will dangle

skull-sized pears & upside
down cross-shaped tubes

filled with cherry-red syrup
already there is a riot of ants

cinching the porch-splattered drops
below they plunge in mawfirst

       they stagger & roll

XXXV

the red–drained center
of the white flower

blooming from
the goat's horn

makes me forget
what I wanted

to see
all of the day

all of me swirls
           down it

XXXVI

each purpleblack disc
of the prickly pear

slumps & slides
toward the dirt

I tie
the boneless flops

to metal stakes
turn the water on

on the other side
of the fence

kids kick a soccer ball
shout ecstatically

there is an ocean
out there beyond

the hollering
the rushing through

red lights
screeching traffic

so many accidents
hose fanning water

over my feet
I listen

to the tiny
failures the world

already is squeezing
            from them

XXXVII

a thousand ripe plums
gape down at me

where squatting
in the dirt I pinch

each beetle pill lady
uncap a jam jar

drop them inside
I love this hot

house smell
sometimes

I forget how
       not to breathe

XXXVIII

splotched among the knotweed
in the boulevard

melting plastic bags
bristle the whistleberry

I backpack the litter
find receipts faded

bottle caps candy
wrappers unopened mail

the wind gusts
when the smur starts

the bags rumple & screech
this is the way

things are
today I want

to be here
my dirt-dark fingertips

       perfectly working

XXXIX

only at dusk does
the city's coppery haze

begin
to unstrangle

my thoughts
we belong to no one

I hum to myself
lightning loves

the live oak
it wishbones

darkness swamps
the overgrown lot

I pass through
bundled

in shadow & duct tape
a statue-still

homeless man
lying flat on his back

fibbers at the purpling sky
to not forget

both of us are singing
the names

of the dead
I know

when we close
our eyes

we share a vision
a lumpy slough

of butchered roosters
over the white tiles

at the room's center
a dreadlock-furred goat

stands tremble-kneed
on a too-bright steel table

bloodshot eyes wide
            open as it bleats

XL

I am again evermore
gone rolling down

the midnight street
scraping parked cars

with my keys a corona
of long dead light

around the stars
my hands climb

the slats of moonglow
there is a tiny & ever

smaller pulse
in my chest

I float the shadows
huck a handcup

of glassy grit
at a blue flickering

window always
it is forever

the perfect moment
to plate our own hearts

on swan smears of fine
        china & begin to feast

XLI

sideways rain
flays through

the already frayed
plum tree

with the power
out

this is the bottom
of the ocean

so the world
is ending

in the murklight
I can see

into my bones
the shine inside them

outside the sgraffitoed eggplant
blisters

each time lightning
Frankensteins

the bruise
      darkening sky

XLII

daylight happens
humming

with need
with slow time

scissored in the back
of my mind

what lies
in the cavern

beneath the ribs
my hand lily white

my hand unfeeling
I know where

pain hellos
in the fractured

light everything
           burns

XLIII

so few worthful
throatings in this

downpour how could it
be that so much time

has passed
the body within

the body the flood
of the flood on

fire & on fire
night sings to me baby

girl tell me you can
handle it all this

is bound
        to be good

XLIV

the black sky
over the park

churns itself bright
over two sodden dogs

that drag zigzag
the empty lawn chairs

they are leashed to
a speechless train

heaves the woods
beyond into a blur

I could die
to the raw-joyed

clattering in that
song last night: scalloped

clouds unbellied
a terrible rain

now: apple cores & wilted
popcorn on the picnic table

across the playground
I pull through

the puddles
I will kiss

the dirt & make it
             bloom

XLV

in the city's long-whispering
leans I feel the barberries

quiver & drop
like buckshot through me

currants in the overgrown
lot long abandoned linger

in the hot-necked wind
the dead shadow

beneath me
is diamond-bodied

its blood is my sweet
blood beautiful

in the sunset trickle

XLVI

toe-skimming the shallows
I cannot stop thinking

about the rising song
mud moans

gusting wind
fingers the eyes

out of the leaf-loose
trees I feel in my gut

deep scratches
on a cherry

wood door
a bone-rattle

the silt clots
the hollows

of my bones
always

there is that racket
all of the hands

I want
to deliver

ribbon wrapped & severed
my own hands shake

as deep as I live
I try to believe

a black spark
lone bird

circles above
updrafting the invisible

      flames of the day

XLVII

I lisp it silken
in the dog grass

murmur throughout
the breaking day

amazed that I am able
to breathe

in all this ghostly wind
go glazed

with the ugliness
of the world

to the edge of the day
to lay all night

with your hands
tendering through

      the buzzsawing dark

XLVIII

a tower of sand dollars
on the window ledge

an egg of moonlight
cradled in the head

of a spoon
past midnight & everyone

sleeps
in the darkest cave

of my body
there is a book

of monsters
it grows

each day a page
all of my dead

singers hackle
the cobwebbed black

I tell the stars
all the beautiful things

they can't know

XLIX

below the ceiling
fan's whirl

this morning
breath

is an oil tanker
with no captain

on the body
a razed town

of bugbites
an unlit bonfire

of fingernails
in the bowl

on the pale floor
from the window

I see two little boys
in the park's shadows

quick-flipping middle fingers
at each other

back & forth
they go

shouting *fuck you*
motherfucker

you're gonna die
bitch

until their rising
laughter convulses

      the entire wet-eyed day

L

around town I wave
at strangers

in crosswalks
all of these lonely

failings draped
over us

it is impossible
to feel

the pearled lightning
in the dirt

through the sidewalks
this concrete blight

croaks no rain ever
             from above

LI

I jumble through
the overgrown kale

leaf beetles
in the mug

of my hand
hummingbirds buzz

the daylight above
from a shadow-swabbed

window I hear a neighbor
yell at the TV

in the sunshine
I wait

for the next cry
the last day that will

come in intensive
care the sickness

each one of us
has but never speaks

of the sun
fingerprints

my closed eyes
each day of this life

     deathmad & beautiful

LII

on the carpet
of the family room

my feet bring
mud

which is a kindness
a prayer

this is it this is it
the rain started

an hour ago
it washed out

my weeping
eyes

they say everything
has happened

or maybe now
nothing at all as

my skin is ice
cold everything is

　　　just fine

LIII

out of the colander
of cut greens

a shimmering blue dot
plummets to the floor

as I crouch to it
I hear whispering

you poor plaything
the beetle pinballs

over the tiles
rolls out

of my grasp
let me show you

the many ways of never
the pecan tree

outside the window
sighs & rubs its hands

your mother your father
I am older now

the world is a terrible place
but I want to last forever

     clinging to its teeth

Acknowledgments

I wish to thank the editors of these magazines for publishing these poems, sometimes in a wildly different shape: *AGNI*, *Grist*, *Connotations Press*, *Ghost Town*, *Laurel Review*, *Los Angeles Review*, *Missouri Review*, *New Republic*, and *Pittsburgh Poetry Review*.

Enormous thanks to all of my colleagues at TCU for their kindness and support—especially the chair of the department of English, Dr. Joddy Murray; Dean Andrew Schoolmaster; and Chancellor Victor Boschini.

To my students—I'm forever grateful for each one of you. Thank you for teaching me so much.

I owe so much to my friends at Milkweed Editions—your incredible support and indefatigable work has helped make all of this possible. Joey—you are amazing with the words! Daniel—you are a true friend.

And with personal gratitude:

To all of my friends in the world of poetry—there are too many of you to list here; my admiration is bottomless. I owe so much to your work, to your energy, to the vibrant heartsongs you fill the pages with. I'm floored by what all of you do. Thank you—I can't wait to see what you do next.

To Casey Golden: I love you, sucka!

To the Balimon family and all its beautiful tendrils—from Pennsylvania to Iowa and Oregon, from Minnesota to Texas and Colorado and Utah—I love you all so much. This book is especially indebted to you.

To Ariane: you are a wonder, so filled with love and compassion for the world we share together. I'm in awe of you. I'm grateful for every second we share in this world that each second of every day we try to make a better place for Felix and Alma. I can't imagine a better way to spend my days—happy, teeming with love, the four of us.

ALEX LEMON is the author of *Happy: A Memoir* and *Feverland: A Memoir in Shards*, and the poetry collections *Mosquito*, *Hallelujah Blackout*, *Fancy Beasts*, and *The Wish Book*. His writing has appeared in *Esquire*, *The Best American Poetry 2008*, *AGNI*, *Gulf Coast*, the *Kenyon Review*, and *Tin House*, among others. He was awarded a literature fellowship in poetry from the National Endowment for the Arts, and he contributes and reviews frequently for a wide range of media outlets. He lives with his wife and two children in Fort Worth, and teaches at Texas Christian University.

milkweed
editions

Founded as a nonprofit organization in 1980, Milkweed
Editions is an independent publisher. Our mission is to
identify, nurture and publish transformative literature,
and build an engaged community around it.

milkweed.org